Desert Tortoise's Burrow

by Dee Phillips

Consultants:

Stephen Hammack
Herpetarium Keeper, St. Louis Zoo, St. Louis, Missouri

Kimberly Brenneman, PhD
National Institute for Early Education Research, Rutgers University, New Brunswick, New Jersey

BEARPORT PUBLISHING

New York, New York

Credits

Cover, © Fuse/Thinkstock, © Anton Foltin/Shutterstock, and © Michael C. Gray/Shutterstock; 2–3, © ZSSD/Minden Pictures/FLPA; 4–5, © Ralph Clevenger/Corbis; 6, © ULKASTUDIO/Shutterstock; 7, © ZSSD/Minden Pictures/FLPA; 8, © Joel Sartore/National Geographic Collection/Getty Images; 9, © ZSSD/Minden Pictures/FLPA, © S. Borisov/Shutterstock, © Kevin M. McCarthy/Shutterstock, © gkuna/Shutterstock, and © pittaya/Shutterstock; 10, © cecoffman/Shutterstock; 11, © David Kuhn/Dwight Kuhn Photography; 12, © Anton Foltin/Shutterstock; 13, © Wayne Lynch/All Canada Photos/Superstock; 14, © James Marvin Phelps/Shutterstock; 15, © George H. H. Huey/age fotostock/Superstock; 16R, © Rick and Nora Bowers/Alamy; 16–17, © Robert Shantz/Alamy; 18, © Glenn and Martha Vargas/California Academy of Sciences; 19, © Stephen Ingram/Animals Animals; 20, © altrendo Nature/Getty Images; 21, © Design Pics/Superstock; 22L, © ZSSD/Minden Pictures/FLPA; 22TR, © George H. H. Huey/age fotostock/Superstock; 22CR, © Robert Shantz/Alamy; 22BR, © David Kuhn/Dwight Kuhn Photography; 23TL, © Wayne Lynch/All Canada Photos/Superstock; 23TC, © Max Topchii/Shutterstock; 23TR, © agap/Shutterstock; 23BL, © Chris Alleaume/Thinkstock; 23BC, © Rosalie Kreulen/Shutterstock; 23BR, © Matt Jepson/Shutterstock.

Publisher: Kenn Goin
Editorial Director: Adam Siegel
Editor: Jessica Rudolph
Creative Director: Spencer Brinker
Design: Emma Randall
Photo Researcher: Ruby Tuesday Books Ltd

Library of Congress Cataloging-in-Publication Data

Phillips, Dee, 1967– author.
  Desert tortoise's burrow / by Dee Phillips.
      pages cm. — (The hole truth!: underground animal life)
  Audience: Ages 7–12.
  Includes bibliographical references and index.
  ISBN-13: 978-1-62724-308-7 (library binding)
  ISBN-10: 1-62724-308-9 (library binding)
 1. Desert tortoise—Behavior—Juvenile literature. 2. Desert tortoise—Habitations—Juvenile literature. 3. Desert tortoise—Life cycles—Juvenile literature. I. Title.
  QL666.C584P45 2015
  597.92'4156—dc23
                                      2014017379

For more information, write to Bearport Publishing Company, Inc., 45 West 21st Street, Suite 3B, New York, New York 10010. Printed in the United States of America.

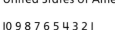

Contents

Meet a Desert Tortoise

It's a sunny morning in a **desert**.

A dusty head pops out from a hole in the ground.

It's a desert tortoise that has been underground all winter.

Now that spring has arrived, the tortoise is leaving its **burrow**.

The hungry animal will search for plants to eat in the warm sunshine.

All About Desert Tortoises

Desert tortoises are closely related to turtles.

Like turtles, tortoises have shells.

Unlike turtles, which live mostly in water, tortoises live only on land.

Tortoises and turtles are members of an animal group called **reptiles**.

All reptiles are cold-blooded.

Their body temperatures rise and drop with the temperature of the air around them.

shell

turtle

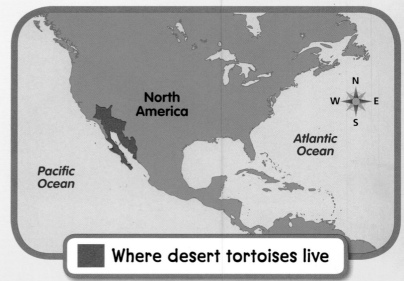

North America

Atlantic Ocean

Pacific Ocean

N
W E
S

Where desert tortoises live

An adult desert tortoise weighs about as much as a cat. Its shell can be up to 15 inches (38 cm) long. Like all reptiles, a desert tortoise has scaly skin.

shell

desert tortoise

How do you think desert tortoises make their burrows?

Digging a Burrow

A desert tortoise builds its burrow in the sandy desert soil.

To make a burrow, a tortoise first digs a tunnel that's up to four feet (1.2 m) long.

It pushes sand aside with its powerful front legs and long claws.

At the end of the tunnel, the tortoise digs a small room.

This will be where it goes to rest and sleep.

desert tortoise foot

claws

A Burrow for Keeping Cool

Desert tortoises live in deserts that are very hot in summer.

To keep from getting too hot, a tortoise spends this time of year underground.

It does not leave its burrow, and it may go without food and water for months.

When the weather gets cooler in the fall, a tortoise spends time above ground.

During the day, it leaves its burrow to search for food.

a desert in summer

In summer, the temperature in a desert can be a super-hot 140°F (60°C)! In winter, it can be freezing.

a tortoise resting in its burrow during summer

What do you think desert tortoises do during winter?

A Burrow for Keeping Warm

When winter comes, the desert gets very cold.

So a desert tortoise spends winter staying warm in its burrow.

All winter, the tortoise rests underground and doesn't eat or drink.

When spring arrives, the desert warms up again.

Now the tortoise spends time during the day searching for food above ground.

a desert in winter

A desert tortoise may dig as many as 12 burrows in the area where it lives. In spring and fall, it walks outside during the day to look for food. When night falls, it sleeps in the nearest burrow.

a tortoise leaving its burrow in spring

Finding Food in the Desert

In spring and fall, a desert tortoise looks for grass and flowers to eat.

It also eats spiky **cacti**, or cactuses, such as prickly pears.

When a tortoise searches for food, it must watch out for danger.

That's because large **predators**, such as coyotes and foxes, may try to eat it.

If a tortoise spots an enemy, it hides in one of its burrows.

coyote

Hiding underground is not the only way that a tortoise stays safe. If a predator attacks it, a tortoise protects its head and legs by tucking them inside its hard shell.

a tortoise eating a
prickly pear cactus

Time to Lay Eggs

In the fall, a male and a female tortoise meet up and **mate**.

By early summer, the female is ready to lay her eggs.

First, she uses her back legs to dig a hole in the ground.

Next, she lays up to 14 round eggs in the hole.

Finally, she covers the eggs with sand to keep them warm and to protect them from predators.

desert tortoise eggs

A desert tortoise egg is about the size of a ping-pong ball.

Tiny Tortoises

Under the sand, the baby tortoises grow inside their eggs.

After about four months, they hatch.

Then the babies dig through the sand and climb up to the surface.

A mother desert tortoise does not take care of her eggs or babies.

Instead, the tiny tortoises must take care of themselves.

Desert tortoises are born with soft shells. It takes about a year for their shells to become hard.

desert tortoise egg

baby tortoise

baby tortoise hatching

A baby tortoise's shell is about 1.6 inches (4 cm) long. On a piece of paper, draw a life-size picture of a baby tortoise. Use a ruler to help you figure out how long its shell should be.

baby desert tortoises

A Tortoise Grows Up

For food, a baby tortoise finds plants to eat.

To keep safe from predators, it hides under plants and rocks.

It also finds shelter in empty burrows dug by adult tortoises.

When it is about five years old, the tortoise is strong enough to dig its own burrows.

Now it is ready to start its grown-up life in the desert!

young desert tortoises hiding under a cactus

adult desert tortoise

By the time it is 15 years old, a desert tortoise is a fully grown adult. It may live to be about 35 years old.

Science Lab

Create a Desert Tortoise Diary

Imagine that you are a scientist studying an adult desert tortoise for a year.

Write a diary about the tortoise's activities using the information in this book.

The tortoise's year can be divided into spring, summer, fall, and winter activities.

Begin the diary with the tortoise leaving its burrow to find food in spring.

Draw pictures to include in your diary, and then present your diary to friends and family.

Read the questions below and think about the answers.

You can include some of the information from your answers in the diary.

Look at the pictures. They will help you, too.

What food does a desert tortoise eat?

Where does a female tortoise lay her eggs?

Why does a tortoise spend the summer and winter months in a burrow?

Science Words

burrow (BUR-oh)
a hole or tunnel dug by
an animal to live in

cacti (KAK-tye) plants
that need little water
to live and usually have
sharp spikes

desert (DEZ-urt) dry land
with few plants and little
rainfall; some deserts are
covered with sand

mate (MAYT) to come
together in order to
have young

predators (PRED-uh-turz)
animals that hunt and
eat other animals

reptiles (REP-tilez)
cold-blooded animals
that have a backbone
and scaly skin

Index

Read More

Blomquist, Christopher. *Desert Tortoises (The Library of Turtles and Tortoises).* New York: PowerKids Press (2003).

Murphy, Julie. *Desert Animal Adaptations (A+ Books).* North Mankato, MN: Capstone Press (2012).

Owen, Ruth. *Sea Turtle Hatchlings (Water Babies).* New York: Bearport (2013).

Learn More Online

To learn more about desert tortoises, visit **www.bearportpublishing.com/TheHoleTruth!**

About the Author

Dee Phillips lives near the ocean on the southwest coast of England. She develops and writes nonfiction and fiction books for children of all ages.